A Note to Parents and Teachers

DK READERS is a comprehensive reading programme for children, designed in conjunction with literacy experts, including Cliff Moon M.Ed., Honorary Fellow of the University of Reading. Cliff Moon has spent many years as a teacher and teacher educator specializing in reading and has written more than 160 books for children and teachers. He is series editor to Collins Big Cat.

Beautiful illustrations and superb full-colour photographs combine with engaging, easy-to-read stories to offer a fresh approach to each subject in the series. Each DK READER is guaranteed to capture a child's interest while developing his or her reading skills, general knowledge, and love of reading.

The five levels of DK READERS are aimed at different reading abilities, enabling you to choose the books that are exactly right for your child:

Pre-level 1: Learning to read
Level 1: Beginning to read
Level 2: Beginning to read alone
Level 3: Reading alone
Level 4: Proficient readers

The "normal" age at which a child begins to read can be anywhere from three to eight years old. Adult participation through the lower levels is very helpful for providing encouragement, discussing storylines and sounding out unfamiliar words.

No matter which level you select, you can be sure that you are helping your child learn to read, then read to learn!

LONDON, NEW YORK, MUNICH,
MELBOURNE AND DELHI

In memory of Joanne Olive Murphy

Series Editor Deborah Lock
Managing Art Editor Rachael Foster
Art Editor Chris Hamilton-Brown
Production Editor Sean Daly
Production Erika Pepe
Illustrator Peter Dennis
Map Illustrator Ed Merritt

Subject Consultant Pamela Petterson,
Information Specialist (retired),
National Historic Oregon Trail
Interpretive Centre

Reading Consultant
Cliff Moon, M.Ed.

Published in Great Britain by
Dorling Kindersley Limited
80 Strand, London WC2R ORL

Copyright © 2008 Dorling Kindersley Limited
A Penguin Company

2 4 6 8 10 9 7 5 3 1
DD449 - 04/08

All rights reserved. No part of this publication may be reproduced,
stored in a retrieval system, or transmitted in any form or by any
means, electronic, mechanical, photocopying, recording,
or otherwise, without the prior written permission
of the copyright owner.

A CIP catalogue record for this book
is available from the British Library

ISBN: 978-1-40533-275-0

Colour reproduction by MDP, UK
Printed and bound in China by L. Rex Printing Co. Ltd.

The publisher would like to thank the following for their kind
permission to reproduce their photographs:
(Key: a=above; b=below/bottom; c=centre; l=left; r=right; t=top)
Alamy Images: John Elk III 32cla, 32tr; Chuck Haney / Danita
Delimont 29tr; Mark Newman / Agency Photo Network 22; Bob
Pardue 15tr; Visual Arts Library (London) 11. **Corbis**: James L.
Amos 27br. **Getty Images**: MPI / Hulton Archive 12. **L.Tom Perry
Special Collections, Harold B. Lee Library, Brigham Young
University, Provo, Utah**: 31tr. **Le Ti Coin Creole - Grill and
Seafood Restaurant**: 32br. **Mary Evans Picture Library**: 25t. **The
Oregon Trail / Boettcher / Trinklein Inc.**: 13tr. **StockFood.com**:
Foodfolio 24crb. **Wikipedia, The Free Encyclopedia**: 16br.
Jacket illustrations: Peter Dennis

All other images © Dorling Kindersley
For more information see: www.dkimages.com

Discover more at
www.dk.com

LUTON LIBRARIES BOROUGH COUNCIL		
938990319		
J 973.5 MUR		PETERS
28-Aug-2008		
- OCT 2008		

DK READERS

Journey of a Pioneer

Written by Patricia J. Murphy

A Dorling Kindersley Book

23 March 1845

Dear Diary,

My name is Olivia Clark and I've lived in Elk Grove, Missouri, USA, my whole life. But that's about to change.

Dad heard that many farming
families are moving west to
Oregon Territory.
They're looking for free,
open land and a new start.
Since times are tough and our
little plot of land can't produce
many crops, we're leaving too.
Dad told us at supper but now
I can't sleep.

Mum said Oregon Territory is far away and it will take many months to get there. Dad warned that we'd travel long distances through wilderness. Sometimes we'll be the only white people around!

The Oregon Trail was a 3,200 km (2,000-mile) path from Missouri to Oregon Territory, passing natural landmarks and crossing rivers. It was used from 1843 to the 1870s.

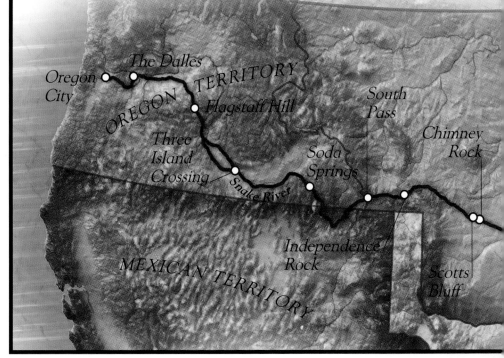

OREGON TERRITORY

Oregon City

The Dalles

Flagstaff Hill

Three Island Crossing

Snake River

South Pass

Chimney Rock

Soda Springs

MEXICAN TERRITORY

Independence Rock

Scotts Bluff

Once we arrive, we'll have a very
large plot of land all to ourselves.
This means a bigger house,
a barn for the animals and
space to grow lots of crops.
I hope I like it there,
wherever *there* is.

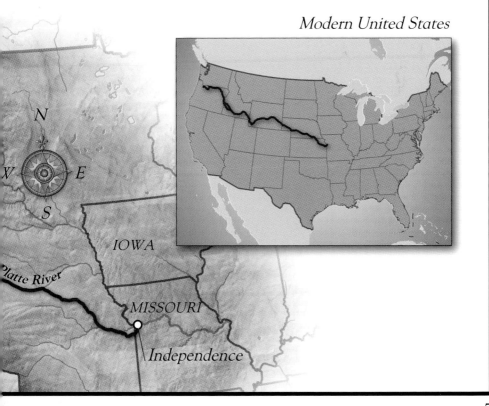

Modern United States

N

W ⊙ E

S

IOWA

Platte River

MISSOURI

Independence

8 April 1845 We've been selling our furniture and anything else that won't fit in our wagon. Mum has filled large barrels with food and packed our cooking tools, china and bedding into a trunk.

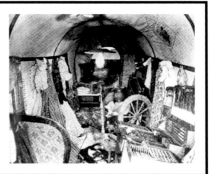

Travelling light
Food took up most of
the room in the small
space inside the wagon.
Many personal items
had to be left behind.

I've packed my doll, Johanna,
but will leave her bed behind.
Dad said that he would build
Johanna another bed when
he makes our new furniture.
He's bought oxen to pull
the wagon.

10 April 1845 Today, we said our last goodbyes. Grandma hugged me so tight I almost stopped breathing.

Friendship in a quilt
Friendship quilts were
a popular parting gift.
Friends sewed their
names onto the quilts'
colourful squares.

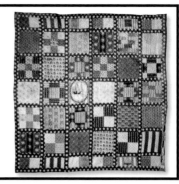

Mum cried when friends gave her
a friendship quilt.
Dad had tears in his eyes, too and
I wondered why everyone was
so sad.
Mum told me later that we might
not see many of these people
ever again.
I didn't want to believe her,
but Mum never lies.

4 May 1845 Today, we reached our "jumping off" point – Independence, Missouri. We bought last-minute wagon supplies here and met up with other people heading west.

Wagons gathering in Independence, Missouri

First traffic jams
With hundreds of
wagons heading west
at one time, slower-
moving wagons caused
long stretches of traffic.

We've split up into groups of
wagons called "trains".
Each train includes men with
important skills, such as doctors,
blacksmiths and builders.
In our train, there is
also a girl
named Lizzie.
She could be
my new best friend.

We've settled into
a daily routine now.
We wake as the sun rises.
Mum makes breakfast and
Dad hitches up the oxen.
We pack up our things
and away we go.

Independence Rock

To avoid travelling in the winter, families hoped to get to Independence Rock, Wyoming, by the Fourth of July.

Most of the day, we walk behind the wagon.

Sometimes, we pick wild flowers.

We travel up to 24 km (15 miles) until night falls – or we fall over!

11 June 1845 We "make camp" when we find a spot with enough grass and water for the oxen.
Dad unhitches the oxen and lets them rest.

I collect dead sagebrush and dried buffalo dung for the fire and help to put up our tent.
Mum makes dinner.

Forming a corral
Each night, the travellers put their wagons in a circle to keep their animals in and wild animals out.

Tonight, we used a tablecloth and
candles as it was Dad's birthday.
For a minute, it felt a little bit
like home.

21 June 1845

After dinner, we clear the table, wash dishes and make beds in the tent.
On special nights, Dad and others play their fiddles and harmonicas.
We sing and dance under the moon.

Most nights, we just want to rest.
I count backwards to get to sleep.
It stops me from wondering how
close the howling animals are.
Men take turns "sitting watch"
to protect the camp.

I try to be brave when we cross rivers, but it can be cold, wet and scary. When the rivers are low, we just walk across. When the rivers are high, we wait until they are lower, and then the oxen pull the wagons across.

If Dad goes hunting, he might
bring back an antelope or catch
a rabbit or a bird for us to eat.
When we find berries,
Mum uses them to make
fresh-baked pies.

Blackberries

Elderberries

After endless prairies, we've finally reached the mountains, but climbing the steep sides is hard work. To go up, we have to lighten our load, which means dumping Mum's stove and trunk.

To get down, we tie rope to a tree and then to the back of the wagon. Then we slowly let out the rope. The Rocky Mountains are too steep. Luckily, we used a flat, wide path through them called South Pass. Oregon Territory is close!

South Pass

South Pass was a 19 km (12-mile) wide trail through the otherwise impassable Rocky Mountains.

On the trail, we have
seen births, celebrated
holidays and marked many
special events.
We have seen tragedy, too.
Some people have become
very ill and died.

Seeing the elephant
Pioneers would say
"I've seen the elephant"
when they met illness
and death along
the trail.

Others have been struck by lightning, shot while hunting, drowned in river crossings and killed by wagons and buffalo. The trail is filled with goodbyes. Today, Lizzie and her family took a different path to get to another part of Oregon Territory. I shall miss her.

After 3,200 km (2,000 miles) and five months of travelling, we've arrived in Willamette Valley, Oregon Territory.

After a few days rest, we picked the plot of land where we'll live and farm.

Once we've built our house, we'll have a big celebration with eating and dancing.

It will take some time to get used to our new life here, but none of us will ever forget our incredible journey along the Oregon Trail.

Pioneer diaries

Historians believe that one in every 250 pioneers kept diaries or journals along the trail, recording their risky journey.

Pioneer facts

In 1805, Meriwether Lewis and William Clark were the first explorers from the United States to reach Oregon Territory. Other explorers, fur trappers, church people and settlers followed afterwards, finding better routes from the east to the west coasts of America.

About 200,000 pioneers travelled west along the Oregon Trail. At first, people used maps and guides to find their way. Later on, they just followed the well-worn ruts from the earlier pioneers' wagon wheels.

Pioneers were called "emigrants". This was because the Oregon Territory was not yet part of the United States. An emigrant is someone who leaves one country and settles in another.

Oregon Territory was later divided into the states of Oregon, Washington, Idaho, small parts of Wyoming and Montana, as well as much of British Columbia, Canada.

Pioneers had fast food, too! Many pioneers' favourite food was the johnnycake, which was like a fluffy pancake. Pioneers could fold them and put them in their pockets until they were ready to eat them.